Road to NAPLAN Success

Phonics and Reading Skills

This book belongs to

....

© 2015 Scholastic Education International (Singapore) Private Limited
A division of Scholastic Inc.

Previously published as Reading & Math Jumbo Workbook Grade K and Grade 1 by Scholastic Inc.

All rights reserved. No part of this publication may be reproduced in whole or in part, or stored in a retrieval system, or transmitted in any form or by any means, electronic, mechanical, photocopying, recording, or otherwise without the written permission of the publisher.

For information regarding permission, write to:
Scholastic Education International (Singapore) Pte Ltd
81 Ubi Avenue 4, #02-28 UB.ONE, Singapore 408830
Email: education@scholastic.com.sg

For sales enquiries write to:
Latin America, Caribbean, Europe (except UK), Middle East and Africa
Scholastic International
557 Broadway, New York, NY 10012, USA
Email: intlschool@scholastic.com

Rest of the World
Scholastic Education International (Singapore) Pte Ltd
81 Ubi Avenue 4, #02-28 UB.ONE, Singapore 408830
Email: education@scholastic.com.sg

Visit our website: www.scholastic.com.sg

This edition 2017

ISBN 978-1-74299-204-4

Welcome to Scholastic Learning Express!

Helping your child build essential skills is easy!
These teacher-approved activities have been specially developed to make learning both accessible and enjoyable. On each page, you'll find:

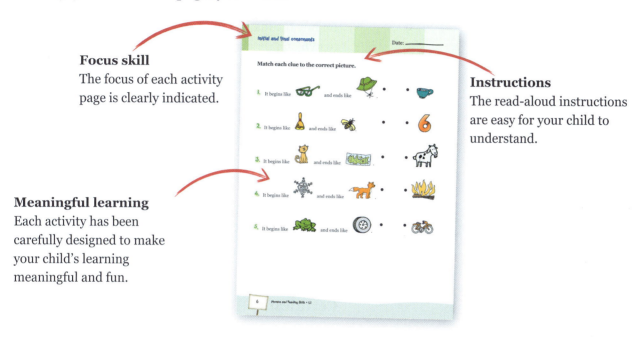

Focus skill
The focus of each activity page is clearly indicated.

Instructions
The read-aloud instructions are easy for your child to understand.

Meaningful learning
Each activity has been carefully designed to make your child's learning meaningful and fun.

This book also contains:

Completion certificate to celebrate your child's leap in learning.

Instant assessment to ensure your child really masters the skills.

Contents

Phonics/Spelling 5
initial and final consonants 6–7
special consonants 8
silent consonants 9
double consonants 10
rhyming words 11–12
sp consonant blend 13
sn consonant blend 14
sm consonant blend 15
st consonant blend 16
tw consonant blend 17
str consonant blend 18
consonant digraphs 19
digraph th 20
digraph sh 21
digraph ch and wh 22
ending digraph ck 23
r-controlled ar 24
r-controlled or 25
spelling list 26
Phonics Spelling Practice Test 27–30

Reading Skills 31
understanding the reading process 32
finding the main idea 33–35
reading for details 36–38
sequencing 39–42
making predictions 43–44
visualising 45–46
classifying 47–49
compare and contrast 50–52
drawing conclusions 53–54
making inferences 55–57
cause and effect 58–60
analyse characters 61–63
reading comprehension 64–73
Reading Skills Practice Test 74–76

Answer Key 77–78
Certificate 79

Phonics/Spelling

Understanding the relationship between letters and the sounds they make, or phonics, is a giant step in learning to read. A good grasp of phonics will help your child become better at spelling.

What to do
The activity pages in this section will give your child practice in identifying and spelling long- and short-vowel sounds, consonant blends, consonant digraphs and rhyming words.

Have your child complete the activities on each page. Review the work together. Praise your child for a job well done.

Keep on going!
Play a phonics/spelling game with your child. Set up word clues and ask your child to say and spell the word. For example:

> I start with the *bl* sound.
> I have a short *-o* vowel.
> I end with the *k* sound.
> I rhyme with stock.
> What word am I? [block]

Have your child give you clues so you can guess the word.

initial and final consonants

Date: _____

Match each clue to the correct picture.

1. It begins like and ends like . • •

2. It begins like and ends like . • •

3. It begins like and ends like . • •

4. It begins like and ends like . • •

5. It begins like and ends like . • •

initial and final consonants

Date: _____

Match each word at the bottom of the page to the word that has the same letters. Write the word in the box. Then write the letters that stand for the beginning and ending sound of each word. The first one has been done for you.

		Beginning Sound	Ending Sound
1.	bus	b	s
	[sub]	s	b
2.	tip	___	___
	[ ]	___	___
3.	ten	___	___
	[ ]	___	___
4.	pal	___	___
	[ ]	___	___
5.	pot	___	___
	[ ]	___	___
6.	gas	___	___
	[ ]	___	___

| top | net | sag | pit | lap | sub |

special consonants

Date: _____

 X *makes the sound of ks. (Hint: Say the word* kiss *very fast!) Most of the time, an* **x** *is in the middle or at the end of a word.*

Help Superhero X put the missing x in each word. Then draw a line to the matching picture.

       fo____

       mi____er

           ta____i

       e____it

           a____e

       si____

           o____

      bo____

           e____ercise

      tu____edo

silent consonants

Date: _____

 Sometimes a consonant may make no sound at all. For example, when k and n come together, the k is silent. When w and r come together, the w is silent. When r and h come together, the h is silent.

Look at the words and pictures. Draw a sleepy eye, like this: above the consonant that is silent. Do not colour it. Then colour the other letters in the word.

double consonants

Date: _____

Read to find out why these children got into trouble. Circle all the double consonants in each sentence. Then find the picture that goes with the sentence. Write the number of the sentence in the correct box.

1. Aki and Jamal giggled in class.
2. Emma and Jenna scribbled on the wall.
3. Hina and Kelly tattled to Mummy.
4. Dai and Kenny held a muddy puppy.

rhyming words

Date: _____

Make your own rhyming words. Look at the picture and say the word. Copy the word. Then change the first letter using each of the letters on the hammer to make new words.

rhyming words

Date: _____

Poems are made with rhyming words. Read the Mother Goose rhymes. Find a word from the box below to rhyme with each underlined word. Copy the word on the line.

1. Jack and <u>Jill</u>

   Went up the _____

   To fetch a pail of water.

   Jack fell <u>down</u>

   And broke his _____,

   And Jill came tumbling after.

2. Hey diddle <u>diddle</u>

   The cat and the _____,

   The cow jumped

   over the <u>moon</u>.

   The little dog laughed

   to see such sport,

   And the dish ran

   away with the _____.

3. Hickory dickory <u>dock</u>

   The mouse ran up the

   _____.

   The clock struck one,

   The mouse ran down

   Hickory dickory dock.

4. Mary had a little lamb,

   Its fleece was white

   as _____.

   Everywhere that Mary went,

   The lamb was sure to <u>go</u>.

Word Box

| fiddle | snow | crown | clock | hill | spoon |

sp consonant blend

Date: _____

 Sp *makes the sound you hear at the beginning of the words* **Spike** *and* **spider**.

Spike the Spider wants to catch sp words in his web. Colour each picture that begins with sp. There are eight of them. Draw a X on the pictures that do not begin with sp.

 This begins with *sp*. It is a green vegetable. It is good for you. Popeye eats it to make him strong. What is it?

sn consonant blend

Date: _____

 Sn *makes the sound you hear at the beginning of the words* **Sniffles** *and* **snake**.

Why is Sniffles the Snake crying? He is lost! Help him find his way back to his mother. First, colour only the pictures that begin with sn. Then use those clues to draw the path to Sniffles' mother.

sm consonant blend

Date: _____

 Sm *makes the sound you hear at the beginning of the words* **Smiley** *and* **Smith**.

Help Smiley Smith find the correct answers. He is looking for one picture in each row that begins with **sm**. Draw a smiley face in each box whose picture begins with **sm**.

1.

2.

3.

Phonics and Reading Skills • L1

st consonant blend

Date: _____

 St makes the sound you hear at the beginning of the words **Stella** and **stars**.

Stella has made up a game for you! Use the star code to make words that begin with st. Write the correct letter above each star. Then draw a line to match each word you made to the correct picture.

1.
2.
3.
4.
5.
6.

tw consonant blend

Date: _____

 Tw makes the sound you hear at the beginning of the words **Twila** and **twins**.

Twila's twins love to ask questions. Read each question below. Find a word from the Word Box that answers the question and write it in the correct call-out.

str consonant blend

Date: _____

 Str *makes the sound you hear at the beginning of the word* **strike**.

Look at the pictures on the caps below. If the picture begins with str, make red stripes on the cap. If the picture does not begin with str, colour the whole cap yellow.

consonant digraphs

Date: _____

 *When two consonants come together and make one new sound, these consonant letters are called **digraphs**.*

Look at the man making new sounds in the digraph machine. He puts in two letters, but only one sound comes out!

Now you try it! Look at the two letters. When the word comes out at the end, draw a green circle around the two letters that make the new sound. That is the digraph!

1. t h — thorn
2. c h — chain
3. w h — wheel

Phonics and Reading Skills • L1   19

digraph th

Date: _____

 The letters **th** make the sound at the beginning of the word **thorn** and **than**.

A. Read each list word. Circle the letters th in each word.

Read.	Copy.	Organise.
		list words that begin with **th**
1. the	_____	
2. this	_____	_____
3. with	_____	_____
4. then	_____	_____
5. bath	_____	_____
6. that	_____	
		list words that end with **th**

Challenge Words

7. them	_____	_____
8. they	_____	_____

B. Write the list word that rhymes with each word.

1. path _____   2. den _____   3. rat _____

Unscramble each list word.

4. het _____   5. hiwt _____   6. tsih _____

20 Phonics and Reading Skills • L1

digraph sh

Date: _____

 The letters **sh** make the sound at the beginning of the word **shell**.

A. Read each list word. Circle the letters sh in each word.

 Read.   Copy.   Organise.

list words that begin with **sh**

1. ship   _____
2. she   _____   _____
3. fish   _____   _____
4. shape   _____   _____
5. wish   _____
6. brush   _____

list words that end with **sh**

_____

Challenge Words

_____

7. shine   _____   _____
8. shoe   _____

B. Draw a shell around the list word that is spelt correctly.

1. shipe   ship   2. shape   shap   3. she   shee

4. fish   fich   5. brosh   brush   6. wich   wish

digraphs ch and wh   Date: _____

> The letters **ch** make the sound at the beginning of the word **chain**.
> The letters **wh** make the sound at the beginning of the word **wheel**.

A. Read each list word. Circle the letters ch and wh in each word.

Read.   Copy.   Organise.

1. chin   _____   list words that begin with **ch**
2. chop   _____   _____
3. whale   _____   _____
4. when   _____   list words that begin with **wh**
5. inch   _____   _____
6. which   _____   _____

Challenge Words   _____

7. why   _____   list words that end with **ch**
8. what   _____   _____

                                          _____

B. Write the list word that rhymes with each word.

1. tail _____   2. mop _____   3. pinch _____

4. pitch _____   5. pen _____   6. win _____

22 Phonics and Reading Skills • L1

ending digraph ck

Date: _____

The letters **ck** make the sound at the end of the word **pick**.

A. Read each list word. Circle the letters ck in each word.

Read.　　**Copy.**　　**Organise.**

list words with short -a sound

1. duck　　_____
2. pack　　_____　　_____　　_____
3. stick　　_____

list words with short -e sound

4. back　　_____　　_____
5. neck　　_____

list words with short -i sound

6. rock　　_____　　_____

Challenge Words

list words with short -o sound

7. clock　　_____　　_____

list words with short -u sound

8. quick　　_____　　_____

B. Write the list word that matches each picture.

1. _____　　2. _____　　3. _____

4. _____　　5. _____　　6. _____

Phonics and Reading Skills • L1   23

r-controlled ar

Date: _____

 *The letters **ar** make the sound at the beginning of the word **arch**.*

A. Read each list word. Circle the letters *ar* in each word.

Read.	Copy.	Organise.
		list words with **ar** in the middle
1. are	_____	
2. hard	_____	_____
3. star	_____	_____
4. jar	_____	_____
5. part	_____	other list words
6. farm	_____	_____
Challenge Words		_____
7. start	_____	_____
8. shark	_____	_____

B. Write the list word that rhymes with each word.

1. card _____   2. art _____   3. harm _____

4. car _____ and _____ and _____

24 Phonics and Reading Skills • L1

r-controlled or

Date: _____

 The letters **or** make the sound at the beginning of the word **ornament**.

A. Read each list word. Circle the letters or in each word.

 Read.   Copy.   Organise.

1. or   _____   two- or three-letter list words
2. corn   _____   _____
3. porch   _____   _____
4. horn   _____   four- or five-letter list words
5. for   _____   _____
6. short   _____   _____

 Challenge Words   _____

7. your   _____   _____
8. horse   _____

B. Write the list word that begins with the same sound as each picture.

1.   2.   3.

4.   5.   6.

spelling list

Throughout the year, see if you can learn all the words in this spelling list.

an	do	if	or	tape
and	dog	inch	pack	ten
are	duck	is	park	that
arm	end	jar	part	the
as	farm	jump	play	then
at	feet	kite	porch	this
ate	fish	let	rain	thorn
back	fly	like	red	to
bath	for	love	rock	top
big	fork	make	rope	tray
black	fox	maths	run	tree
bone	from	me	see	up
brush	gave	men	seed	wait
bug	get	mud	shape	we
but	go	my	she	whale
by	got	nail	ship	when
cake	had	name	shop	which
came	hand	neck	short	white
can	hard	need	sit	wish
car	hat	nine	six	with
chin	him	north	so	yes
chip	his	nose	star	you
chop	home	not	stay	
corn	hop	note	stick	
day	horn	of	sun	
dish	I	on	tail	

Fill in the circle next to the correct answer.

1. Which word has the **silent k sound**?

   - A knife
   - B kite
   - C kit
   - D kind

2. Which word has the **silent w sound**?

   - A wind
   - B write
   - C white
   - D weak

3. Which word does NOT have a digraph sound?

   - A chain
   - B cap
   - C thin
   - D ship

Fill in the circle next to the correct answer.

4. Which word rhymes with **love**?

   ○ A   come

   ○ B   from

   ○ C   dove

   ○ D   some

5. Which word rhymes with **high**?

   ○ A   fright

   ○ B   sight

   ○ C   sigh

   ○ D   night

6. Which word answers the following riddle?
   I shine in the sky. What am I?

   ○ A   Mars

   ○ B   star

   ○ C   Earth

   ○ D   Saturn

Fill in the circle next to the correct answer.

7. Which word does NOT have a digraph sound?

   ○ A   fish

   ○ B   find

   ○ C   rack

   ○ D   whale

8. Which word rhymes with **kind**?

   ○ A   mine

   ○ B   find

   ○ C   fine

   ○ D   child

9. Which word rhymes with **start**?

   ○ A   lit

   ○ B   part

   ○ C   step

   ○ D   line

Phonics and Reading Skills • L1

Fill in the circle next to the correct answer.

10. Which word does NOT have the **sn consonant blend**?

    ○ A   star

    ○ B   snow

    ○ C   sneeze

    ○ D   snip

11. Which word has the **sm consonant blend**?

    ○ A   snail

    ○ B   smoke

    ○ C   ship

    ○ D   skip

12. Which word has the **tw consonant blend**?

    ○ A   thick

    ○ B   tip

    ○ C   twelve

    ○ D   sweet

Reading Skills

In this section, your child reviews previously learnt reading skills and is introduced to new ones. These essential skills will help your child better comprehend what he or she is reading.

What to do
Read each page with your child. Then have him or her complete the activities. Be sure to review your child's work.

Keep on going!
Have your child choose a book and read it together. Start by asking your child to look at the cover of the book. Have him or her predict what the story will be about based on the cover picture. Next, while reading, stop every few pages and ask questions: Where did the story take place? Describe the main characters. What do you think will happen next? What problem does the main character face? How is the problem solved? Can you retell the story in your own words? This process is called active reading. Good readers are active readers!

understanding the reading process

Date: _____

Tim is a good reader. He uses clues to help him read. First, he looks at the pictures. That helps him know what the story is about. Next, he reads the title of the story. Now he knows a little more. As he reads the story, the words make pictures in his mind.

Colour in the book beside the correct answer.

1. Who is Tim?

    a good reader   a maths champion

2. What does Tim do first?

    reads the story   looks at the pictures

3. What else helps Tim know what the story will be about?

    the title   the page number

4. As he reads, what makes pictures in Tim's mind?

    the letters   the words

finding the main idea

Date: _____

 The **main idea** tells what the whole story is about.

Today I went to the circus. My favourite part of the circus was the clowns. Clowns can do funny tricks. A clown named Pinky turned flips on the back of a horse. Fancy Pants juggled balls while he was singing a funny song. Happy Hal made balloons into animal shapes. Then twelve clowns squeezed into a tiny car and rode away.

Colour in the ball that tells the main idea.

- Clowns drive tiny cars.
- Balloons can be shaped like animals.
- Pinky rides a horse.
- Clowns can do funny tricks.
- Fancy Pants sang a song.

finding the main idea

Date: _____

Trucks do important work. Dump trucks carry away sand and rocks. Cement trucks have a barrel that turns round and round. They deliver cement to workers who are making footways. Fire engines carry water hoses and firefighters. Oil is delivered in large tankers. Flatbed trucks carry wood to the people who are building houses.

Find the sentence in the story that tells the main idea. Write it in the circle below. Then draw a line from the main idea to all the trucks that are described in the story.

Phonics and Reading Skills • L1

finding the main idea

Date: _____

When you were born, your parents thought of a name for you. You might be named after someone in the family. Maybe you were named after a film star! Almost every name has a meaning. Pamela means "made from honey". Henry means "master of the house". Ellen means "bright". Sometimes, books about baby names tell the meanings. Many of the meanings will surprise you!

A. Circle the name below that has the main idea of the story in it.

B. To find out the meanings of the names in the puzzle below, follow each string of beads. Copy the letters on each bead in order in the boxes.

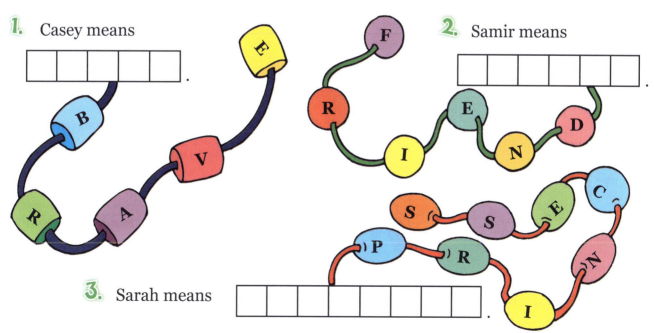

1. Casey means ☐☐☐☐☐.

2. Samir means ☐☐☐☐☐☐.

3. Sarah means ☐☐☐☐☐☐☐☐.

Phonics and Reading Skills • L1   35

reading for details

Date: _____

➤ **Details** *are parts of a story. Details help you understand what the story is about.*

Skunks are small animals that live in the woods. They have black fur with one or two white stripes down their backs. Insects, fruits and nuts are their favourite food. They also eat mice. If a skunk raises its tail, run away! Skunks can spray a very smelly liquid at anyone who bothers them.

Write the answers in the crossword puzzle.

Across

2. What colour are the stripes on a skunk's fur?

5. What is a skunk's favourite food apart from insects and fruits?

Down

1. What is another thing that skunks like to eat?

2. Where do skunks live?

3. What does a skunk raise when it is getting ready to spray?

4. What should you do if a skunk raises its tail?

 Use details to describe your favourite animal.

reading for details

Date: _____

Ricky loved to go camping. One day during reading class, he began to daydream about camping in the mountains. He thought about going fishing and riding horses. It would be fun to gather logs to build a campfire and cook hot dogs. He and his dad could set up the tent near some big trees. He wished he were in his canoe right now. Just then, Ricky heard his teacher say, "Ricky, it is your turn to read." Oh no! He had lost the place!

Circle these things from the story hidden in the picture below: a fish, a fishing pole, a log for the campfire, a hot dog, a tree and a canoe.

1. Where was Ricky during this story? _____

2. Where would Ricky like to have been? _____

Phonics and Reading Skills • L1   37

reading for details

Date: _____

Kelly is going to spend the night with her grandmother. She will need to take her nightdress, a shirt and some shorts. Into the suitcase go her toothbrush, toothpaste and hairbrush. Grammy told her to bring a swimsuit in case it was warm enough to swim. Mum asked her to pack her favourite pillow and storybooks. Dad said, "Don't forget to take Grammy's sunglasses that she left here last week." Now Kelly is ready to go!

Colour the things that Kelly packed in her suitcase.

 A compound word is a big word that is made up of two small words. For example, cow + boy = cowboy. Find nine compound words in this story and circle them.

sequencing

Date: _____

 Sequencing *means putting the events in a story in the order that they happened.*

Last summer, I learnt how to swim. First, the teacher told me to hold my breath. Then, I learnt to put my head under water. I practised kicking my feet. While I held on to a float, I paddled around the pool. Next, I floated to my teacher with my arms straight out. Finally, I swam using both my arms and my legs. I did it! Swimming is fun! This summer, I want to learn to dive off the diving board.

Number the pictures in the order that they happened in the story.

Unscramble the letters to tell what the boy in the story wants to do next.

EALNR   OT   IVDE

___ ___ ___ ___ ___   ___ ___   ___ ___ ___ ___

Phonics and Reading Skills • L1

sequencing

Date: _____

1. **Read the story.**

   My mother gave me some seeds. I dug some holes in the garden.
   I planted the seeds.
   Each day I watered the seeds. I waited for a few weeks to go by. Soon some flowers began to grow.

2. **Read the sentences below. Rewrite them in the correct order.**

   Some flowers began to grow.
   I planted the seeds.
   My mother gave me some seeds.
   I watered the seeds.

   1. _____
   2. _____
   3. _____
   4. _____

sequencing

Date: _____

1. **Read the story.**

   Tomorrow I will go swimming. I will put on my swimsuit. I will jump in the water to get wet. Then I will dive off the diving board. Grandma will make lunch for me. Mum will swim with me after lunch.

2. **Read the sentences below. Rewrite them in the correct order.**

   Mum will swim with me.
   I will put on my swimsuit.
   Grandma will make lunch for me.
   I will jump in the water.

1. _____

2. _____

3. _____

4. _____

Phonics and Reading Skills • L1   41

sequencing

Date: _____

1. **Read the story.**

   Dad and I went fishing today. We woke up very early. We ate breakfast. We left the house after we ate. We went to the bait shop. Dad bought some worms. We caught five fish. Mum was happy to cook them for us.

2. **Read the sentences below. Rewrite them in the correct order.**

   We ate breakfast.
   Dad bought some bait.
   We woke up early.
   Mum cooked our fish.

   1. _____
   2. _____
   3. _____
   4. _____

making predictions

Date: _____

 Use story details to make a guess about what will happen next.

Mia and Rosa were playing hospital. Mia was the patient and Rosa was the doctor. Rosa pretended to take Mia's temperature. "You have a fever," she said. "You will have to lie down." Mia climbed onto the top bunk bed. "You need to sleep," Dr Rosa said. Mia rolled over too far and fell off the top bunk. "O-o-o-h, my arm!" yelled Mia. Her mother came to look. It was broken!

What do you think happened next? Write your answer here.

_____

To find out if your answer is correct, finish the sentence below by colouring only the spaces that have a dot in them.

Mia had to go to

making predictions

Date: _____

One day, Sam was riding his bike to a baseball game. He had to be on time. He was the pitcher. Just ahead, Sam saw a little boy who had fallen off his bike. His knee was bleeding and he was crying. Sam asked him if he was okay, but the boy couldn't speak English. Sam knew the boy needed help getting home. If he stopped to help, he might be late for the game. Sam thought about it. He knew he had to do the right thing.

What do you think Sam did next? There are two paths through the maze. Draw a line down the path that shows what you think Sam did next.

Which sentence from the story gives you a hint about what Sam decided to do? Write that sentence below.

_____

visualising

Date: _____

 Picturing a story can help the reader understand it better.

An artist drew the pictures that are in this book. Now it is your turn to be the artist! Read each sentence very carefully. Draw exactly what you read about in the sentence.

1. The green-and-yellow striped snake wiggled past the ants.

2. Wild flowers grew along the banks of the winding river.

3. On her sixth birthday, Shannon hung streamers and balloons on the walls.

visualising

Date: _____

Big, black clouds appeared in the sky. Lightning struck the tallest tree. The scared cow cried, "Moo!" It rained hard. Soon there was a mud puddle by the barn door. Hay blew out of the barn window.

Read the story above. Then go back and read each sentence again. Add to the picture everything that the sentences describe.

classifying

Date: _____

 Grouping like things together makes it easier to remember what you read.

Mum says, "Let's go out for ice-cream! Clean your room, and then we will go." Your room is a mess. You need to put the blocks in the basket. The crayons must go in their box. The books must go on the shelf, and the marbles go in the jar. You can do it. Just think about that hot-fudge sundae!

Draw a line from each item on the floor to the place it belongs. Colour the things that you could use in school red. Colour the toys blue.

Circle the food that does not belong in an ice-cream shop.

classifying

Date: _____

 Look for similarities when grouping items.

Read the words in the Word Box. Write each word in the place where you would find these things at the shopping mall.

Word Box

tickets	sandals	high heels	beans	big screen
tulip bulbs	peppers	fertiliser	popcorn	gardening gloves
shoes	burritos	boots	flowerpots	sweets	tacos

1. Sandie's Shoe Shop

2. Film Town Cinema

3. PEPE'S MEXICAN FOOD

4. Gale's Gardening Goodies

48   Phonics and Reading Skills • L1

classifying

Date: _____

Eating good food helps you grow up to be strong and healthy. There are many kinds of foods. Fish, chicken and beef are meats. Dairy foods include milk, cheese and yogurt. What kinds of bread do you like? I like muffins, bagels and biscuits. Fruits and vegetables, such as carrots, corn and apples, are good for you. They are full of vitamins.

Look at the pictures of different foods below. Draw a line from each food to the category it belongs to.

| Meats | Dairy | Breads | Fruits and Vegetables |

Phonics and Reading Skills • L1   49

compare and contrast

Date: _____

 Compare *means to look for things that are the same.*
Contrast *means to look for things that are different.*

To solve the riddles in each box, read the clues in the horse. Then write the letters in the blanks with the matching numbers.

What kind of food does a racehorse like to eat?

___ ___ ___ ___   ___ ___ ___ ___
11   5   10   3   11   9   9   2

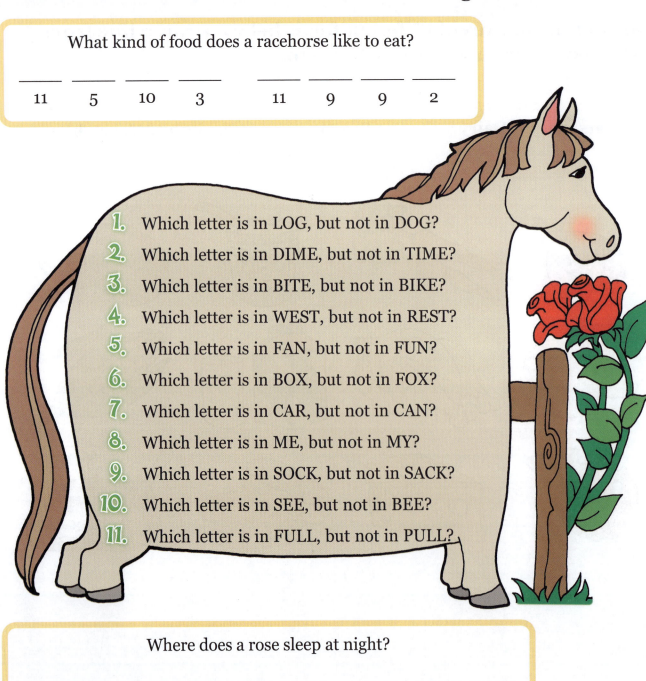

1. Which letter is in LOG, but not in DOG?
2. Which letter is in DIME, but not in TIME?
3. Which letter is in BITE, but not in BIKE?
4. Which letter is in WEST, but not in REST?
5. Which letter is in FAN, but not in FUN?
6. Which letter is in BOX, but not in FOX?
7. Which letter is in CAR, but not in CAN?
8. Which letter is in ME, but not in MY?
9. Which letter is in SOCK, but not in SACK?
10. Which letter is in SEE, but not in BEE?
11. Which letter is in FULL, but not in PULL?

Where does a rose sleep at night?

___ ___ ___ ___ ___ ___   ___ ___ ___
11   1   9   4   8   7   6   8   2

compare and contrast

Date: _____

Holly and Polly are twins. They are in Year 1. They look alike, but they are very different. Holly likes to play softball and football. She likes to wear her hair braided when she goes out to play. She wears sporty clothes. The playground is her favourite part of school. Polly likes to read books and paint pictures. Every day she wears a ribbon in her hair to match her dress. Her favourite thing about school is going to the library. She wants to be a teacher some day.

Look at the pictures of Holly and Polly. Their faces look alike. Circle the things in both pictures that are different from each other.

Draw two lines under the words that tell something about Holly and Polly that is the same.

They play sports.   They love to paint.   They are in Year 1.

compare and contrast   Date: _____

Juan's dad and Ann's dad are soldiers. Juan's dad is a captain in the Navy. He sails on the ocean in a large ship. Ann's dad is a pilot in the Air Force. He flies an aeroplane. Juan and Ann miss their dads when they are gone for a long time. They write them letters and send them pictures. It is a happy day when their dads come home!

Draw a ☺ in the column under the correct dad. Some sentences may describe both dads.

		Juan's dad	Ann's dad	Both dads
1.	He is a captain.			
2.	He works on a ship.			
3.	Sometimes he is gone for a long time.			
4.	He is a pilot.			
5.	His child writes to him.			
6.	He is in the Air Force.			
7.	He is in the Navy.			
8.	It is a happy time when he comes home.			
9.	He flies an aeroplane.			
10.	He is a soldier.			

drawing conclusions

Date: _____

 When you use your own thoughts to answer the question "How could that have happened?", you are **drawing conclusions**.

I bought a fancy carpet today. It was made of brightly coloured yarn. I placed it on the floor in front of the television and sat on it. All of a sudden, it lifted me up in the air! The carpet and I flew around the house. Then out the door we went. High above the trees, we soared like an eagle. Finally, the carpet took me home and we landed in my backyard.

How could that have happened? To find out, use your crayons to trace over each line. Use a different colour on each line. Write the letter from that line in the box at the bottom of the rug.

Could this story really happen? Draw a carpet around your answer.

Yes   No

drawing conclusions

Date: _____

Have you ever heard a parrot talk? Parrots are able to copy sounds that they hear. You can train a parrot to repeat words, songs and whistles. But a parrot cannot say words that it has never heard. People can use words to make new sentences, but a parrot cannot.

Read each sentence. If it is true, colour the parrot under True. If it is false, colour the parrot under False.

		True	False
1.	You could teach a parrot to sing "Happy Birthday".	🦜	🦜
2.	You could ask a parrot any question, and it could give the answer.	🦜	🦜
3.	A parrot could make up a fairy tale.	🦜	🦜
4.	If a parrot heard your mum say, "Brush your teeth," every night, he could learn to say it, too.	🦜	🦜
5.	It is possible for a parrot to repeat words in Spanish.	🦜	🦜

54 Phonics and Reading Skills • L1

making inferences

Date: _____

 When you use what you know to make a decision, you are making an inference. Use details from the story to make decisions about the characters.

Circle the picture that answers the riddle.

1. I am a female. I like to watch films and listen to music. My grandchildren love my oatmeal biscuits. Who am I?

2. I live in the ocean. I swim around slowly, looking for something to eat. I have six more arms than you have. Who am I?

3. I am a large mammal. I live in the woods. I have fur. I stand up and growl when I am angry. Who am I?

4. I am an insect. If you touch me, I might bite you! I make tunnels under the ground. I love to come to your picnics! Who am I?

5. I have feathers. I also have wings, but I don't fly. I love to swim in icy water. Who am I?

making inferences

Date: _____

 Use story details to help you make decisions about the story.

James was the first boy in Miss Lane's class to find red spots on his face and arms. He scratched until his mum came to take him home. A week later, Amy and Jana got the spots. The next Monday, six more children were absent. Finally, everyone got well and came back to school. But this time, Miss Lane was absent. Guess what was wrong with her!

Colour red spots on the correct answers.

1. What do you think was wrong with the children?

sore throats   chickenpox   broken arms

2. How do you know the spots were itchy?

James scratched them.

Amy said, "These spots itch!"

3. How many children in all got sick?

2   5   9   4

4. Why do you think Miss Lane was absent? Write your answer.

_____

_____

making inferences

Date: _____

Read the sentence below each picture. In the call-outs, write what each character could be saying.

Mr Giraffe asked Mr Zebra why he had stripes. Mr Zebra didn't know.

Mr Giraffe said that he should ask Mrs Owl. Mr Zebra agreed.

Mr Zebra asked Mrs Owl why he had stripes. Mrs Owl laughed.

Mrs Owl told Mr Zebra that the Magic Fairy had painted him that way!

cause and effect

Date: _____

 *In a story, there is usually a reason something happens. This is the **cause**. What happens as a result is the **effect**.*

Sandy went on a holiday in the mountains with her parents and little brother Austin. They were staying in a small cabin without any electricity or running water. It was fun to have lanterns at night and to bathe in the cold mountain stream. The biggest problem for Sandy was she missed her best friend, Kendra. Sandy found her dad's mobile phone and called Kendra. They talked for nearly an hour! When Sandy's dad wanted to call his office, the mobile phone was dead. He was NOT a happy camper!

Draw a line to match the first part of each sentence to the second part that makes it true.

1. Sandy used lanterns at night because

2. Sandy bathed in a stream because

3. Sandy felt better about missing Kendra because

4. Sandy's dad could not call his office because

- she talked to her on the mobile phone.
- the cabin had no running water.
- the cabin had no electricity.
- the mobile phone was dead.

cause and effect

Date: _____

It is important to follow the rules at school.

Read each rule below. Find the picture that shows what would happen if students did not follow that rule. Write the letter of the picture in the correct box.

1. You must walk, not run, in the halls. ☐

2. Do not chew bubblegum at school. ☐

3. Come to school on time. ☐

4. When the fire alarm rings, follow the leader outside. ☐

5. Listen when the teacher is talking. ☐

6. Keep your desk clean. ☐

cause and effect

Date: _____

 In a story, there is usually a reason something happens. This is the **cause**. What happens as a result is the **effect**.

Wanda Wiggleworm was tired of living alone in the flowerpot, so she decided to enjoy herself. Last night, Wanda went to the Ugly Insect Ball. She looked her best, all slick and slimy. Carl Caterpillar asked her to dance. They twisted and wiggled round and round to the music. All of a sudden, they got tangled up. They tried to get free, but instead, they tied themselves in a knot! What could they do? They decided to get married and they lived happily ever after.

Unscramble each sentence about the story. Write the new sentence on the line.

1. tangled | worms | when | got | danced. | they | The | up

_____

_____

2. in | knot | They | married. | a | they | were | so | got | tied

_____

_____

analyse characters

Date: _____

 A character is a person or animal in a story. To help readers understand a character better, a story often gives details about the character.

Once upon a time, there was a mixed-up queen named Margie. She got things mixed up. She wore her crown on her arm. She wore a shoe on her head. She painted every fingernail a different colour. Then she painted her nose red! She used a fork to hold her hair in place. She wore a purple belt around her knees. The king didn't mind. He always wore his clothes backwards!

Use the story and your crayons to help you follow these instructions:

1. Draw Margie's crown.
2. Draw her shoe.
3. Paint her fingernails and nose.
4. Draw what goes in her hair.
5. Draw her belt.

Circle the correct answer:

6. What makes you think Margie is mixed up?

    the way she dresses

    the way she talks

7. What makes you think the king is mixed up, too?

    He talks backwards.

    He wears his clothes backwards.

analyse characters

Date: _____

I love Miss Ticklefoot. She is my Year 1 teacher.

To find out more about her, read each sentence below. Write a word from the Word Box in each blank that tells how she feels.

Word Box

| sad | scared | silly | worried | happy | surprised |

1. Miss Ticklefoot smiles when we know the answers.
   _____

2. She is concerned when one of us is sick.
   _____

3. She makes funny faces at us during lunchtime.
   _____

4. She cried when our fish died.
   _____

5. She jumps when the fire alarm rings.
   _____

6. Her mouth dropped open when we gave her a present!
   _____

Phonics and Reading Skills • L1

analyse characters

Date: _____

When Ty was four years old, he had two make-believe friends named Mr Go-Go and Mr Sasso. They lived in Ty's cupboard. When there was no one else around, Ty talked to Mr Go-Go while he played with his toys. Mr Go-Go was a good friend. He helped put Ty's toys away. Mr Sasso was not a good friend. Some days he forgot to make Ty's bed or brush Ty's teeth. One day, he even talked back to Ty's mother. Another day Dad said, "Oh my! Who wrote on the wall?" Ty knew who did it … Mr Sasso!

Read the phrase inside each crayon. If it describes Mr Go-Go, colour it green. If it describes Mr Sasso, colour it red. If it describes both, colour it yellow.

1. helpful
2. probably cheeky
3. forgets to do chores
4. friends that live in the closet
5. could get Ty in trouble
6. make-believe characters
7. does the right thing

Draw Mr Go-Go.

Draw Mr Sasso.

reading comprehension

Date: _____

Read the story and then answer the questions.

My Uncle's Aeroplane

My uncle has a new aeroplane. It is yellow with blue stripes. The wings have stars on them. It flies high. He took me on a trip in his new aeroplane. The name of his aeroplane is *Yellow Bird*.

1. Who has a new aeroplane?

2. What are the colours of the aeroplane?

3. What are on the wings of the aeroplane?

4. Who took a trip in the new aeroplane?

5. What is the name of the aeroplane?

6. Does the aeroplane fly high or low?

reading comprehension

Date: _____

Read the story and then answer the questions.

If I Were King

I would like to be a king. I would wear a robe with diamonds on it. I would wear a gold crown on my head. I would call the land I rule "Funville". Every year we would have a parade. I would want all the people in Funville to be happy.

1. What would I like to be?
   _____
   _____

2. What would be on my robe?
   _____
   _____

3. What would I wear on my head?
   _____
   _____

4. What would I call my land?
   _____
   _____

5. What would happen every year in Funville?
   _____
   _____

6. Do I want the people in Funville to be happy?
   _____
   _____

reading comprehension

Read the story and then answer the questions.

Joel's Pets

Joel has three pets. He has two cats and one dog. Joel's cats are named Fifi and Foofoo. Joel's dog is named Hook. Joel gives his pets fresh food and water each day. He plays fetch with Hook.

1. How many pets does Joel have?

2. How many cats does Joel have?

3. How many dogs does Joel have?

4. What are the names of Joel's cats?

5. What is the name of Joel's dog?

6. What does Joel give to his pets?

reading comprehension

Read the story and then answer the questions.

Larry the Frog

Larry is a frog. Larry is green with brown spots. He loves to play in the pond. Sometimes Larry catches flies. He likes to eat flies for dinner. After Larry catches flies, he hops around the pond.

1. What is Larry?

2. What colour is Larry?

3. Where does Larry love to play?

4. What does Larry catch?

5. What does Larry like to eat for dinner?

6. What does Larry do after he catches flies?

Read the story and then answer the questions.

Karen's Doll

Karen's favourite toy is her doll. The doll's name is Kathy. Kathy has blonde hair and wears a pink dress. Karen was three years old when she got her doll. Kathy sleeps on Karen's bed when Karen is at school.

1. What is Karen's favourite toy?

2. What is the name of Karen's doll?

3. What colour is Kathy's hair?

4. What colour is Kathy's dress?

5. What does Kathy do when Karen is at school?

6. Is Kathy a real person?

Read the story and then answer the questions.

Chris Likes Science

My name is Chris. I like to read. I like stories about stars and planets the best. The book I am reading now is about the sun. The book has many pictures. It has a picture of the sun on the cover. We will study the sun in science class next year.

1. What is my name?

2. What kind of books do I like?

3. What am I reading about now?

4. What does the book I am reading have a lot of?

5. What is on the cover of this book?

6. What will I study next year at school?

Read the story and then answer the questions.

Rainy Day

Roy likes to play in the rain. When it rains, he puts on his raincoat and boots. He goes outside. Roy splashes in the puddles. Roy must think that he is a duck. Sometimes Meyer plays in the rain with Roy.

1. What does Roy like to play in?

2. What does Roy put on when it rains?

3. Where does Roy go?

4. What does Roy splash in?

5. What must Roy think he is?

6. Who plays in the rain with Roy sometimes?

Read the story and then answer the questions.

Rowe's Dog

My friend Rowe has a dog. I really like Rowe's dog. His dog is brown. She wears a red collar. Rowe plays with the dog a lot. Rowe's dog loves to chew on bones. I wish I had a dog like Rowe's.

1. What does my friend Rowe have?

2. Do I like Rowe's dog?

3. What colour is Rowe's dog?

4. What colour is the dog's collar?

5. What does Rowe's dog chew on?

6. What do I wish?

Read the story and then answer the questions.

Baby Chickens

A mother chicken sat in her nest. She was a big chicken with yellow feathers. She was sitting on some eggs. One day, the eggs cracked open. Then some little chicks popped out of the eggs. Now the chicken had six chicks.

1. Where did the mother chicken sit?

2. What colour were her feathers?

3. What was the mother chicken sitting on?

4. What happened to the eggs one day?

5. What came out of the eggs?

6. How many chicks were there?

reading comprehension

Read the story and then answer the questions.

Wally the Whale

Wally is a big, blue whale. Wally lives in the ocean. He swims with his whale friends. Sometimes Wally dives deep and then jumps high into the air. When he lands in the water, Wally makes a big splash.

1. What kind of animal is Wally?

2. What colour is Wally?

3. Where does Wally live?

4. Who does Wally swim with?

5. What does Wally do after he dives deep?

6. What happens when Wally lands in the water?

Reading Skills Practice Test

Fill in the circle next to the sentence that tells about each picture.

Example

- ● A   A girl sits.
- ○ B   A girl walks.
- ○ C   A girl runs.
- ○ D   A girl eats.

1.
- ○ A   The boy plays ball.
- ○ B   The cat plays.
- ○ C   The girls run and play.
- ○ D   The cat runs.

2.
- ○ A   The book is on the desk.
- ○ B   He has two books.
- ○ C   The pen is next to the book.
- ○ D   The book is on the chair.

3.
- ○ A   We have a big bag.
- ○ B   She has a rabbit.
- ○ C   He has a rug and a pan.
- ○ D   She has a cat.

4.
- ○ A   Six donkeys sit.
- ○ B   The dog sits on a hill.
- ○ C   A goat plays in the mud.
- ○ D   A cat climbs a tree.

Phonics and Reading Skills • L1

Reading Skills Practice Test

Read the story and answer each question. Fill in the circle next to the best answer.

Pam has a dog. His name is Rags.
Rags likes to play.
Rags likes to run.
Rags likes to jump.
Rags is a good dog!

5. What kind of pet does Pam have?

   ◯ A   cat
   ◯ B   dog
   ◯ C   rabbit
   ◯ D   gerbil

6. What is a good title (name) for this story?

   ◯ A   Rags the Dog
   ◯ B   Frogs Jump
   ◯ C   Apples Grow on Trees
   ◯ D   Pam has a Bad Dog

7. What does Rags like to do?

   ◯ A   skip
   ◯ B   play
   ◯ C   sing
   ◯ D   eat

Phonics and Reading Skills • L1   75

Fill in the circle next to the correct answer.

8. What letter is in PAT, but not CAT?

   ○ A   P
   ○ B   C
   ○ C   A
   ○ D   T

9. Fill in the circle next to the event that comes first.

   ○ A   Sue eats a piece of cake.
   ○ B   Mum opens the cake mix.
   ○ C   Sue adds eggs and milk to the mix.
   ○ D   Mum puts the mix in a bowl.

10. Fill in the circle that answers the riddle.

    I am an insect.
    I bite people.
    People don't like me.
    I leave red marks on people.
    Who am I?

    ○ A   a slug
    ○ B   a mosquito
    ○ C   a ladybird
    ○ D   a grasshopper

Answer Key

Phonics/Spelling

Page 6
1. goat   2. bike   3. cup
4. six   5. fire

Page 7
2. tip, t, p; pit, p, t 3. ten, t, n; net, n, t 4. pal, p, l; lap, l, p 5. pot, p, t; top, t, p 6. gas, g, s; sag, s, g

Page 8
Review that directions have been followed and matching lines have been drawn.

Page 9
Review that beginning k, w and h have sleepy eyes above and remaining letters are coloured.

Page 10
Circle: gg, ss; mm, nn, bb, ll; ll, tt, mm; nn, dd, pp; 3, 2, 4, 1

Page 11
hand: sand, land, band
ball: hall, call, mall, tall, wall, fall
dog: fog, jog, log, hog
cat: pat, sat, rat, mat, fat, hat, bat

Page 12
1. hill, crown   2. fiddle, spoon
3. clock   4. snow

Page 13
Colour: spear, spoon, sponge, spill, spur, spaghetti, spaceship, spider
Cross: bike, lamp, hat, horse, compass; spinach

Page 14
Colour: snowflake, snowman, snorkel, snap, snail, sneeze, snout

Page 15
1. smoke   2. smile   3. smell

Page 16
1. stamp   2. stork   3. starfish
4. stapler 5. stick   6. stove

Page 17
1. Twirl!   2. Twelve   3. Twister
4. Tweezers 5. Tweet! Tweet!
6. Twenty

Page 18
red: 1, 2, 3, 4, 5, 6, 9, 11
yellow: 7, 8, 10, 12

Page 19
1. th   2. ch   3. wh

Page 20
A. begin with th: the, this, then, that; end with th: bath, with
B. 1. bath   2. then   3. that
   4. the   5. with   6. this

Page 21
A. begin with sh: ship, she, shape; end with sh: fish, wish, brush
B. 1. ship   2. shape 3. she
   4. fish   5. brush 6. wish

Page 22
A. begin with ch: chin, chop; begin with wh: whale, when, which; end with ch: inch, which
B. 1. whale 2. chop   3. inch
   4. which 5. when   6. chin

Page 23
A. a: pack, back; e: neck; i: stick; o: rock; u: duck
B. 1. neck   2. duck   3. stick
   4. rock   5. pack   6. back

Page 24
A. ar in the middle: hard, part, farm; other words: are, star, jar
B. 1. hard   2. part   3. farm
   4. are, star, jar

Page 25
A. 2–3 letter: or, for;
   4–5 letter: corn, porch, horn, short
B. 1. short 2. porch 3. corn
   4. horn   5. or   6. for

Page 26
Review that directions have been followed.

Page 27–30
1. A   2. B   3. B   4. C
5. C   6. B   7. B   8. B
9. B   10. A   11. B   12. C

Reading Skills

Page 32
1. a good reader
2. looks at the pictures
3. the title
4. the words

Page 33
Clowns can do funny tricks.

Page 34
Trucks do important work.
Dump truck, cement truck, fire engine, tanker, flatbed truck

Page 35
A. KATE
B. 1. brave   2. friend   3. princess

Page 36
Across	Down
2. white	1. mice
5. nuts	2. woods
	3. tail
	4. run

Page 37

1. reading class
2. camping in the mountains

Page 38
Colour: nightdress, shirt, shorts, toothbrush, toothpaste, hairbrush, swimsuit, pillow, storybooks, sunglasses

Page 39
6, 4, 2, 3, 1, 5;
LEARN TO DIVE

Page 40
1. My mother gave me some seeds.
2. I planted the seeds.
3. I watered the seeds.
4. Some flowers began to grow.

Page 41
1. I will put on my swimsuit.
2. I will jump in the water.
3. Grandma will make lunch for me.
4. Mum will swim with me.

Page 42
1. We woke up early.
2. We ate breakfast.
3. Dad bought some bait.
4. Mum cooked our fish.

Page 43
Review the prediction;
Mia had to go to a real hospital.

Page 44
Review the prediction;
He knew he had to do the right thing.

Page 45–46
Review that directions have been followed.

Page 47
Review lines and colouring;
red: books, crayons; blue: blocks, marbles;
sandwich

Page 48
1. sandals, high heels, shoes, boots
2. tickets, big screen, popcorn, sweets
3. beans, peppers, burritos, tacos
4. tulip bulbs, fertiliser, gardening gloves, flowerpots

Page 49
meats: fish, chicken, beef
dairy: yogurt, milk, cheese
breads: bagels, muffins, biscuits
fruits and vegetables: carrots, corn, apple

Page 50
fast food;
1. L 2. D 3. T 4. W
5. A 6. B 7. R 8. E
9. O 10. S 11. F;
flower bed

Page 51
Circle: hair, clothes, socks, shoes, bat/ball, paintbrush/book;
They are in Year 1.

Page 52
1. Juan's dad 2. Juan's dad
3. Both dads 4. Ann's dad
5. Both dads 6. Ann's dad
7. Juan's dad 8. Both dads
9. Ann's dad 10. Both dads

Page 53
It was a flying carpet. Review that directions have been followed.

Page 54
1. True 2. False 3. False
4. True 5. True

Page 55
1. grandmother 2. octopus
3. bear 4. ant
5. penguin

Page 56
1. chickenpox
2. James scratched them.
3. 9
4. She got chickenpox, too.

Page 57
1. Giraffe: Why do you have stripes?
   Zebra: I don't know.
2. Giraffe: You should ask Mrs Owl.
   Zebra: Yes.
3. Zebra: Why do I have stripes?
   Owl: Ha Ha Ha.
4. Owl: The Magic Fairy painted you that way!

Page 58
1. the cabin had no electricity.
2. the cabin had no running water.
3. she talked to her on the mobile phone.
4. the mobile phone was dead.

Page 59
1. E 2. B 3. D 4. F
5. A 6. C

Page 60
1. The worms got tangled up when they danced. 2. They were tied in a knot so they got married.

Page 61
1–5. Review that directions have been followed.
6. the way she dresses
7. He wears his clothes backwards.

Page 62
1. happy 2. worried 3. silly
4. sad 5. scared 6. surprised

Page 63
1. green 2. red 3. red 4. yellow
5. red 6. yellow 7. green

Page 64
1. uncle 2. yellow and blue
3. stars 4. me/the author
5. Yellow Bird 6. high

Page 65
1. a king 2. diamonds
3. gold crown 4. Funville
5. a parade 6. yes

Page 66
1. three 2. two 3. one
4. Fifi and Foofoo 5. Hook
6. fresh food and water

Page 67
1. a frog
2. green with brown spots
3. in the pond 4. flies 5. flies
6. He hops around the pond.

Page 68
1. her doll 2. Kathy 3. blonde
4. pink 5. sleeps on Karen's bed
6. no

Page 69
1. Chris
2. stories about stars and planets
3. the sun
4. pictures
5. a picture of the sun
6. the sun

Page 70
1. the rain 2. raincoat and boots
3. outside 4. puddles 5. a duck
6. Meyer

Page 71
1. a dog 2. yes 3. brown 4. red
5. bones 6. to have a dog like Rowe's

Page 72
1. in her nest 2. yellow 3. eggs
4. they cracked open 5. chicks
6. six

Page 73
1. a whale
2. blue
3. in the ocean
4. his whale friends
5. he jumps high into the air
6. he makes a big splash

Page 74–76
1. B 2. A 3. B 4. B
5. B 6. A 7. B 8. A
9. B 10. B

Congratulations!

Scholastic Learning Express

I, _____ am a Scholastic Superstar!

I have completed Phonics and Reading Skills L1.

Presented on _____

Paste a photo or draw a picture of yourself.